ᐊᒃᓴᓅᓚᐅᕐᓂᖅ ᐅᒡᔫᑉ ᕿᔪᐊᓂᒃ

MAKING ROPE OUT OF BEARDED SEALSKIN

ᐅᖃᓕᒫᒐᓕᐅᖅᑑᒃ
ᓲᓴᓐ ᐊᒻᒪ
ᐃᓕᓴᐱ ᐊᕕᙵᖅ
ᑎᑎᖅᑐᒐᖅᑎ
ᓚᐊᓂ ᓚᓯᓐᑯ

WRITTEN BY
Susan and
Elisapee Avingaq
ILLUSTRATED BY
Lenny Lishchenko

ᐃᓄᐃᑦ ᐊᑐᓵᖑᕗᑦ ᕿᓯᖕᓂᒃ
ᓱᓇᒃᑯᑖᓕᐊᕆᓪᓗᒋᑦ, ᒪᑯᓂᖓ ᐊᓐᓄᕌᓂᒃ
ᐱᓇᓱᑎᓂᓪᓗ. ᐅᓪᔫᑦᑕᐅᖅ ᕿᓯᖓ
ᐊᒃᖢᓈᓕᐊᖑᓵᖑᒋᕗᖅ.

Inuit use sealskin to make many things, such as clothing and tools. One thing you can make out of sealskin is rope.

ᐊᒃᖢᓈᑦ ᐊᑐᕐᓂᖃᖅᑐᒻᒪᕆᐊᓘᕗᑦ. ᓇᐳᓯᐅᑎᑎᒋᔾᐅᕙᓚᐅᖅᐳᑦ ᖃᒧᑏᒃ ᓇᖅᑭᑕᖅᕕᖏᓐᓄᑦ ᓇᖅᑭᑕᕈᑕᐅᔅᓗᑎᓪᓗ. ᐃᐸᕋᐅᑕᓯᐊᖑᔪᓐᓇᖅᐳᑦ, ᐊᓗᓯᐊᖑᔪᓐᓇᖅᐳᑦ ᑲᒦᖕᓄᑦ, ᐊᒻᒪᓗ ᐊᔾᒐᓚᖏᓐᓂᒃ ᐊᑐᖅᑕᐅᔪᓐᓇᖅᐳᑦ.

Rope is a very useful tool. It is used to make a *qamutiik* and to tie things onto a qamutiik. It can also be used as a whip for dogsledding, for the soles of *kamiik*, and many other things.

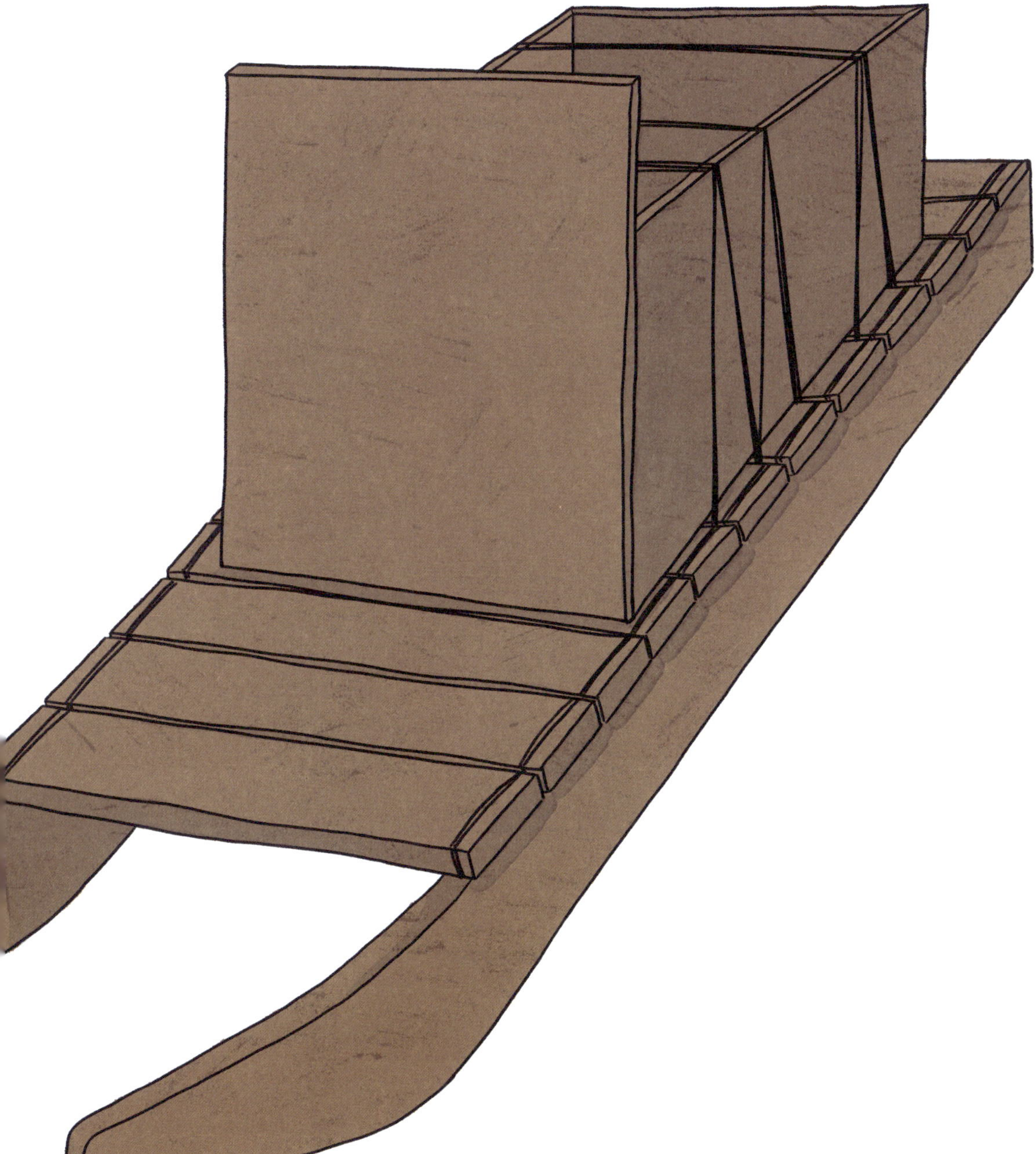

ᐃᒫᒃ ᑕᕝᕙ ᐊᒃᓱᓈᓕᐅᕈᓐᓇᖅᐳᑎᑦ ᐅᒡᔫᑉ ᕿᓯᖕᒐᓂᒃ. ᐅᒡᔪᑦ ᐃᔾᔪᔪᐊᓗᖕᒥᒃ ᕿᓯᖅᑲᖅᐳᑦ, ᐊᒃᓱᓈᒃᓴᑦᑎᐊᕙᐅᒐᓪᓗ.

This is how you make rope out of sealskin from a bearded seal. Bearded seals have tough skin, so it is good for making rope.

ᐱᓕᕆᐊᖑᓂᖓ 1:

ᓯᕗᓪᓕᖅᐹᒥᒃ, ᕿᓯᒃ ᐊᒡᕕᖕᒥ **ᐅᖅᓱᖓ** **ᒪᔾᔭᒡᓗᒍ**. ᐊᒡᕕᑦ ᓵᑦᑐᓵᖑᕗᑦ ᕿᐅᖅᑐᕐᕕᐅᓪᓗᑎᒃ ᕿᓯᖕᓂᒃ.

Step 1:

First, put the thick strip of skin through an *agvik* and scrape the **blubber** off. An agvik is a slanted table used for skinning.

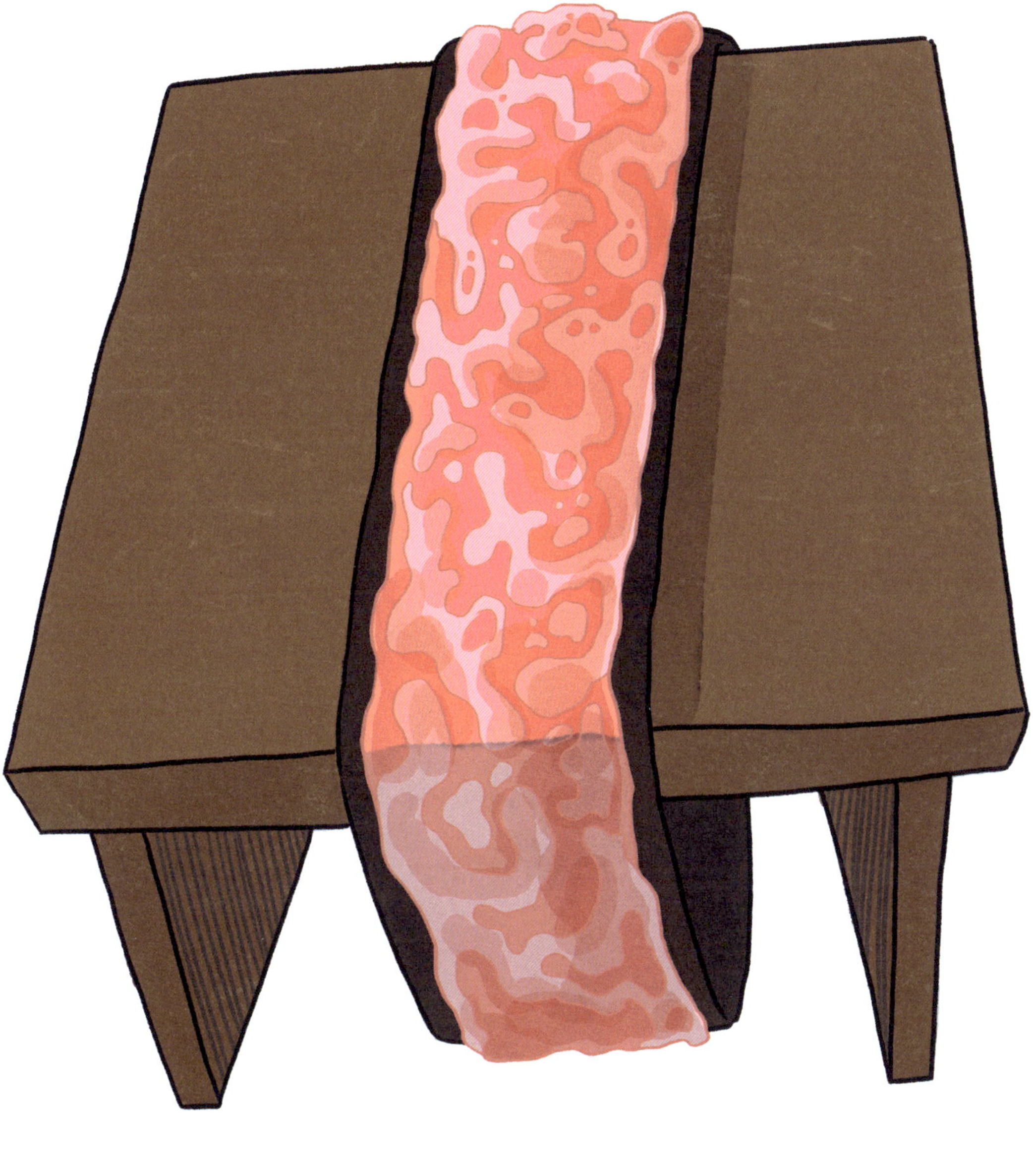

ᐱᓕᕆᐊᖑᓂᖓ 2:

ᐅᓗᒧᑦ ᒥᖅᑯᖓ ᒫᔾᔭᒡᓗᒍ.

ᐃᓚᖏᑦ ᒥᖅᑯᐃᔭᐃᓲᖑᙱᓚᑦ ᐊᒃᖢᓅᓕᐅᖅᖢᑎᒃ. ᐃᓚᖏᑦ ᒥᖅᑯᐃᔭᐃᓲᖑᔪᑦ.

Step 2:

Then use an *ulu* to scrape off all the fur.

Some people use a skin with the fur on. Some people scrape the fur off. When people scrape fur off the skin, it's called "*majjak.*"

ᐱᓕᕆᐊᕐᕈᓂᖓ 3:

ᐅᖅᓱᐃᔭᕇᖅᐸᑦ, ᑭᓕᒡᓗᒍ ᑕᑭᒡᓕᑎᑦᓗᒍ. “ᑭᓕᖕᓂᕋᐃᓲᖑᕗᑦ,” ᕿᓯᖕᒥᒃ ᐊᒃᓱᓈᓚᐅᖅᑐᑦ ᖁᐱᑯᑖᒡᓗᒍ.

Step 3:

After you finish scraping the blubber off, cut the skin into a long strip. Cutting the skin into a long strip is called *“kili.”*

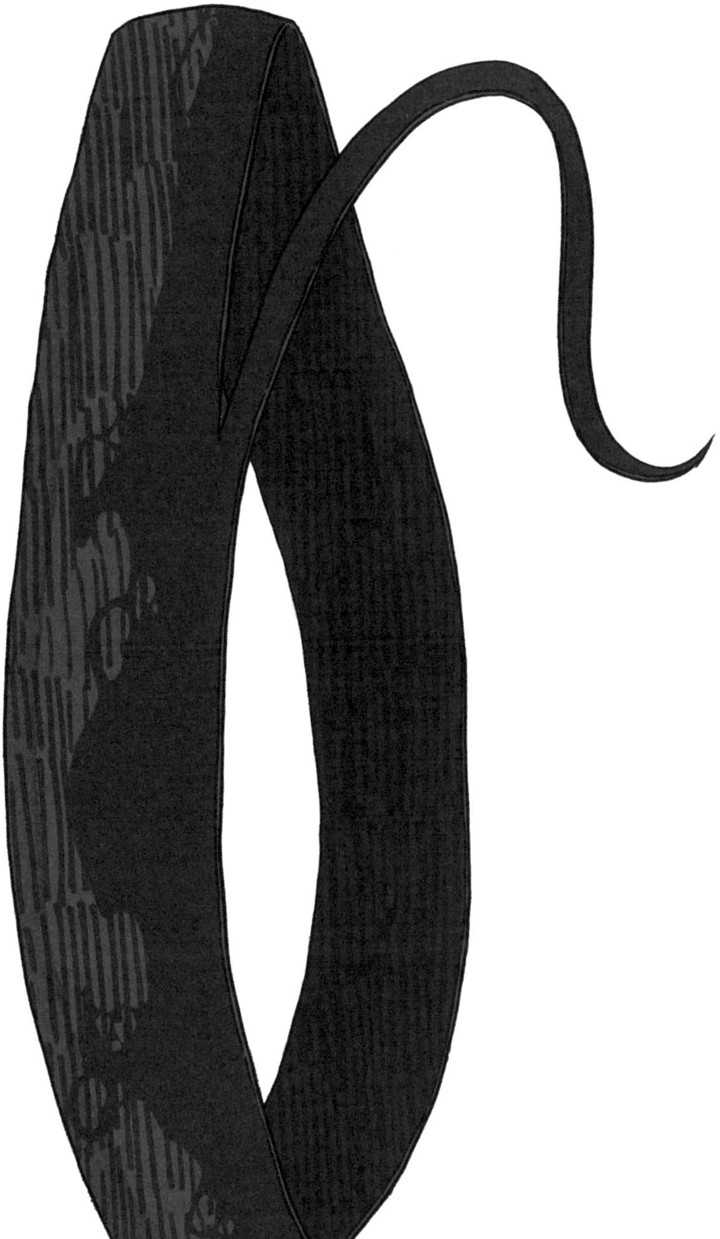

ᐃᑲᔪᖅᑲᑎᒌᒃᑑᖕᓄᑦ ᑭᓚᖕᓂᖅᑕᐅᓱᖕᒍᕗᖅ ᐅᓪᔫᑉ ᕿᓯᖕᒪ.

ᐊᑕᐅᓯᖅ ᑎᒍᒻᒥᓲᖕᒍᕗᖅ ᕿᓯᖕᒥᒃ ᓱᖃᖓᑎᒥᐊᖅᓗᒍ. ᑖᓐᓇ "ᑎᒍᓯᔫᓂᖅᑕᐅᕗᖅ."

ᐊᐃᑉᐸᖓ ᓴᕕᖕᒥᓄᑦ ᑭᓚᓲᖕᒍᕗᖅ ᖁᐱᑯᑖᖅᓗᒍ ᐊᒃᓗᓈᓚᐊᖅ.

It takes two people to cut the skin.

One person holds the skin. This person is called "*Tigusijuq*."

The other person uses a knife to cut the skin into a strip.

ᐱᓕᕆᐊᖑᓂᖓ 4:

ᐊᒻᒪᐃᓛᒃ, ᐊᒃᔪᕌᓕᐊᑉ ᐃᓱᖏᒃ ᐱᑐᒃᑕᐅᓲᖑᕘᒃ ᐅᔭᕋᖕᓄᑦ ᑕᓯᑦᑎᐊᖅᓯᒪᓪᓗᓂ.

Step 4:

Next, tie each end of the strip of skin to a big rock.

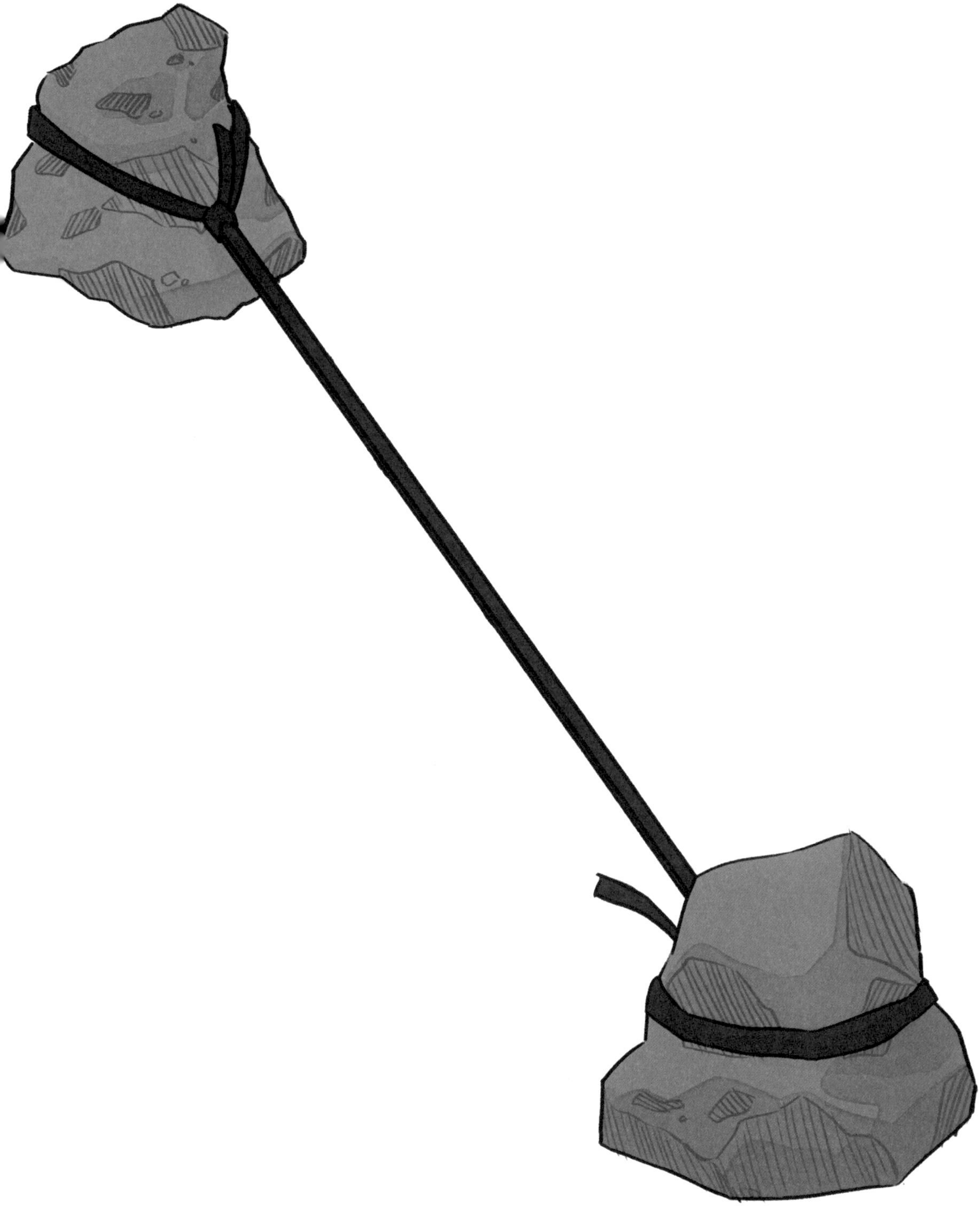

ᐱᓕᕆᐊᖑᓂᖓ 5:

ᐋᖅᓱᖅᓂᕋᖅᑕᐅᓕᓲᖑᒍᖅ ᐊᒃᓗᓈᓕᐊᖅ ᑕᒪᓐᓇ **ᐊᒥᕋᐃᔭᖅᑕᐅᑦᑐᓂ** ᓯᓂᖓᑐ ᐊᖕᒪᑐᖅᑕᙳᖅᑕᐅᑦᑐᓂ.

ᐆᒃᑕᔫᒧᑦ ᐋᖅᓱᕆᓐᓇᖅᐳᑎᑦ. ᐆᒃᑕᔫᖅ ᐃᐱᒃᓴᖅᓯᒪᑦᑎᐊᕆᐊᓕᒃ ᐋᖅᓱᖅᑐᓂ.

Step 5:

Now you can *aaqsuq*. That means taking the **membrane** off and smoothing the edges to make the rope.

You can use a pocket knife to aaqsuq. The knife needs to be very sharp.

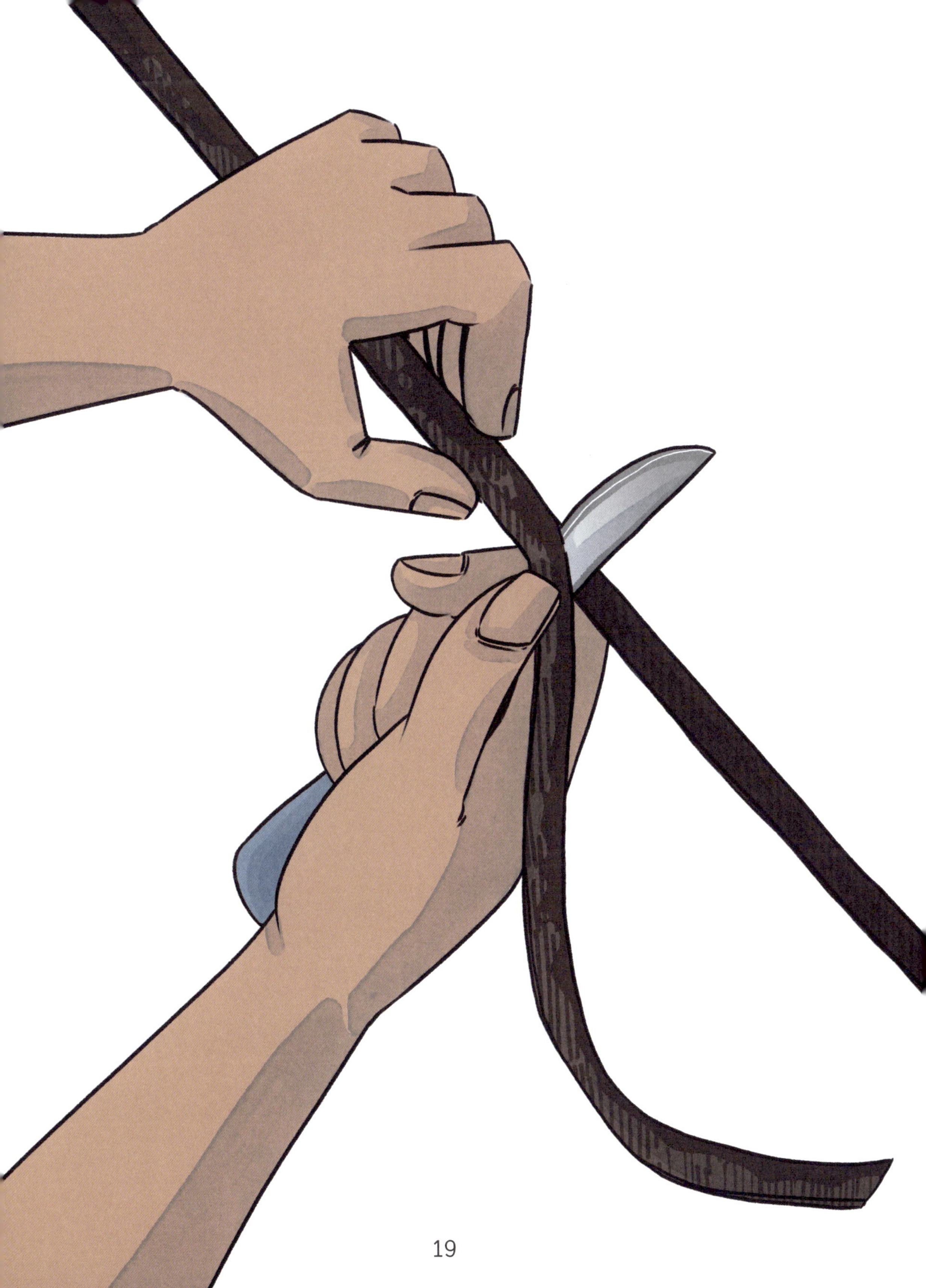

ᐱᓕᕆᐊᖑᓂᖓ 6:

ᐊᒃᕈᓈᓕᐊᖅ ᐋᖅᓱᕐᓂᖓᓂ, ᒥᖅᑯᐃᔭᖅᑕᐅᔪᓐᓇᖅᐳᖅ ᐆᒃᑕᕉᕐᒍᑦ. ᓯᓂᓕᒫᖓ ᑎᓇᖅᑯᐃᔭᕐᓗᒍᓗ.

Step 6:

While you aaqsuq, you can use a sharp knife to take the fur off if you didn't beforehand in step 2. Then smooth out the edges.

ᐱᓕᕆᐊᖑᓂᖓ 7:

ᑖᒃᑯᓂᖓ ᐱᐊᓂᒃᑯᕕᑦ, ᐊᒃᓱᓈᓕᐊᖅ ᓂᕙᙵᒍᕐᑐᒍ ᐸᓂᖅᓯᐊᕆᓕᕐᑐᒍ.

ᑕᐃᒫᒃ ᑕᕝᕙ ᐊᒃᓱᓈᓕᐊᖑᓲᖑᒐᑦ ᐅᒡᔫᑉ ᖅᑭᓯᖓᓂᒃ.

Step 7:

When you are done, hang the rope to dry.

That is how you make bearded sealskin rope.

ᐅᖃᐅᓯᑦ ᑐᑭᖏᑦ

ᐅᖅᓱᖅ
ᐸᐃᓘᑦ ᕿᐅᔾᔭᐃᒃᑯᑎᖏᑦ ᐃᒪᕐᒥ.

ᒪᔾᔭᒃ
ᐅᖅᓱᐃᔭᐃᔪᖅ ᐅᓗᒧᑦ ᐸᐃᓗᐅᑉ ᕿᓯᖓᓂᒃ ᒪᔾᔭᒃᐳᖅ.

ᒪᒥᖅ
ᐸᐃᓘᑦ ᕿᓯᖏᑕ ᐅᖅᓱᐊᓄᑦ ᐊᒃᑐᐊᓂᖓ ᐃᕿᔮᑖ; ᑐᒃᑑᑉ ᐊᒥᖓᑕ ᓂᕿᐊᓄᑦ ᐊᒃᑐᐊᓂᖓ.

Glossary

blubber
a layer of fat beneath the skin of sea mammals.

membrane
a thin layer of skin.